How to Make Your Partner Sexually Satisfied

David Paragon

TABLE OF CONTENT

INTRODUCTION

STEP BY STEP INSTRUCTION TO MAKE YOUR PARTNER PHYSICALLY FUFILLED

Some of the significance of sex in marriage.

Incredible sex starts with great correspondence.

Keep away from schedule.

Foreplay: stretch it out.

Try not to fear hot talk.

Toys: not the sort for kids.

Share your dreams.

Be GGG.

SECTION 1

We are not brought into the world with a natural limit with regards to extraordinary sex right from the outset of our sexual lives

Recollect whenever you first were physically personal with your accomplice. It presumably didn't make the earth shift on its pivot, correct? That is totally ordinary. Assuming you are considering how to have great sex with a lady or how to fulfill a man in bed then realize that extraordinary sex is learned. How about we perceive how to instruct ourselves, all while playing around with some great sex!

Incredible sex starts with great correspondence

Sexual accomplices can't guess each other's thoughts so the tips on the most proficient method to fulfill your man in bed all emphasis on bunches of talking. Indeed! Sharing what you like and could do without is fundamental data for your accomplice to have so he can understand what you really want to raise you to indescribable state of ecstasy of good sex. Furthermore, you don't need to hold on until you are sleeping to communicate your longings... discussing sex over mixed drinks or a cozy supper can be important for foreplay; it's a genuine turn on, regardless of whether you can't try all that you are proposing immediately. At the point when you are having intercourse, don't be modest about telling your join forces with words, instead of simply thankful groans, what feels better. "I love it when you contact me there," or "gracious indeed, continue to do that," is exceptionally useful in conveying to your accomplice precisely what you really want regarding great sex. Could it be said that he is accomplishing something you don't see as wonderful? Instead of simply brushing away his hand without fail and afterward figuring how to fulfill your man, let him know verbally: "Gracious, could you at any point concentrate somewhat more here and not there?"

All kinds of people find it exceptionally energizing when their accomplices let them know they are near climax. "I'm nearly there, don't stop!" can be exceptionally useful so that the man could hear, as in some cases they aren't as fixed on the female climax as they may be (since the signs are not really self-evident) so they love to know when it is working out (and this excites them extraordinarily).

Stay away from schedule

Assuming you and your accomplice have gotten into a sexual daily schedule, having intercourse that very night every week or consistently similarly situated, eventually you will observe that that sort of sex is dull. To make sex extraordinary once more, change everything around and perceive how physically fulfilled that makes you.

How to fulfill your significant other assuming he prefers doing likewise sexual thing over and over? Have intercourse unexpectedly — do it in the first part of the prior day going to work, or spend Saturday evening in bed investigating one another. What about in an alternate piece of the house (ensure the youngsters aren't anywhere near!)? Could leaving some apparel on, say, your skirt or pullover, causing it to appear as though you just couldn't hold on to get your hands on one another? Attempt various positions or a few situations throughout the span of the night for a decent sex to shock your accomplice. Is your man normally the person who assumes responsibility for the lovemaking? Change that up! You start, you direct, and you make major decisions. (He'll cherish this!)

Foreplay: stretch it out

Great sex isn't just about how to fulfill your better half in bed yet stepping up to the plate and make the experience something so magnificent that you go off the deep end simply contemplating it the following time! Presently men appear to be ready to switch promptly into "sex mode," however for ladies, they need additional opportunity to move. An extraordinary method for getting the temperament hot is to focus on the foreplay, even the "previously" foreplay. Assuming you realize that you will have intercourse tonight, send each other a provocative message during the day to begin the foreplay a long time before you return home to clear a path for some smoking' great sex. Let each know other how you intend to treat each other's bodies once you hit the sheets. Your messages will send the message that you are extremely centered around what the night will bring, which will increase your craving message by instant message.

When you are home, there's compelling reason need to race to the room. The point is to wait in the foreplay second... perhaps taking your dress off piece by piece in the parlor, or beginning with a shoulder rub in the foyer, moving your hands to additional fascinating puts on your accomplice's body while still upstanding. Bother one another. Move towards intercourse gradually, with however much limitation that you can gather. You will see that when entrance happens, it won't be simply great sex. It will be mind boggling!

Try not to fear provocative talk

Utilizing provocative jargon while having intercourse is a colossal turn-on, particularly for men. On the off chance that you are modest about utilizing specific words, begin with those you are OK with. At the point when you are contemplating how to fulfill your significant other in bed, you might feel that not so much talk but rather more work might be the way yet attempt some provocative talk and see the distinction.

Toys: not the sort for youngsters Sex toys are an incredible method for accomplishing sexual fulfillment. Now that they are out in the standard, an ever-increasing number of couples are integrating them into their sex play for profoundly fulfilling sex. Begin by taking a gander at an index or a site together, and sharing your thought process may be great to attempt, and why you are drawn to that toy instead of another. Glancing through the determination of toys is an extraordinary method for telling your accomplice your inclinations and what you really want to get you to climax, notwithstanding what your accomplice is as of now doing. The women as a rule may not consider utilizing toys in any event, when they are a misfortune to comprehend how to fulfill spouse physically yet all it needs is only a psyche that is available to numerous conceivable outcomes. Share your dreams

Hello yet my man could do without toys or the messy talk so how to satisfy my significant other physically, a spouse wonder. Difficult task without a doubt however at that point it's not difficult to remove him from the safe place. Paying attention to your accomplice's mystery dreams, and sharing your own with him, can assist with expanding his drive and sexual fulfillment as well as yours. Keep in mind: dreams are definitively that. It doesn't imply that you or he would truly wish to do these things, in actuality. The way that they could never really happen is important for the sensuality behind letting each know other what you fantasize about while thinking about great sex. GGG Might it be said that you are known about the abbreviation GGG? It represents great, giving and game. If you have any desire to physically fulfill one another, you will need to make being GGG an objective. Great you are great in bed; you appreciate sex and anticipate your personal minutes with your accomplice. Giving you are liberal in bed, focusing on your accomplice's pleasure. Game you are ready for attempting new things and being available to your accomplice's ideas and solicitations for making your sexual coexistence fulfilling, hot and invigorating. Attempt new things no less than once (for however long you are alright with them). No one can tell when that "a certain something" will be something that turns you on such a lot of that it will end up being an ordinary component in your lovemaking meetings. Great sex isn't excessively complicated. It simply takes two individuals to truly be at the time, cut the tedium with amazements and consider new ideas (and the bed!). There's nothing more to it! As yet considering how to fulfill a man in bed physically or how to deeply inspire a lady with great sex, then, at that point, begin step by step with these tips and see the distinction.

SECTION 2

Whether you've been hitched for 10 days or 10 years, sexual fulfillment is likely a quite huge piece of your relationship

Furthermore, to do your part to guarantee your accomplice is basically as fulfilled as could really be expected, what's truly significant? Correspondence! All things considered, you won't ever be aware without a doubt on the off chance that he's fulfilled or not except if you inquire. However, talking is just important for it — you additionally need to completely finish what you discussed in the room (which ought to be the tomfoolery part). Here, you'll find

a few hints and deceives that will assist you fabricate a physically satisfying relationship with your better half that fulfills you both.

1.Tell him to what lengths you will go for him. A recent report showed feeling wanted is significant for men's sexual fulfillment. For by far most of the ones who partook in the review (an astounding 95%), "feeling wanted" positioned as vital. Some even said it meant quite a bit to them than fundamental actual requirements like eating and dozing. The least demanding method for assisting him with feeling wanted is to tell him whether it's eye to eye or through a provocative little text.

• For instance, you could message him as he's coming back from work and express something like, I've been pondering your body close to mine. I ache for your touch.

• While you two are out together, you could incline close and murmur in his ear, I failed to remember how hot you search in that suite I simply need to eat up you.

2. Contact him consistently in non-sexual ways. (A) Heartfelt touch causes him to feel cherished and wanted. Maybe you recall when you and your better half initially begun dating and you were unable to keep your hands off one another. Diverting a portion of that energy into your wedded life will assist with expanding his sexual and by and large fulfillment in the relationship.

• This could be pretty much as unobtrusive as a light touch on his arm as you're talking or a concise press as you brush past him in the kitchen. Lay your hand on his arm as you're perusing something together or on his leg when you're in the vehicle.

• Recall how you could contact somebody when you were playing with them and attempting to stand out, then touch your significant other in a portion of the same ways. Similar looks and looks work as well! A momentary, significant look can cause him to feel the same way your hand brushing his chest or waiting on his arm would.

• Kissing and nestling in bed around evening time, regardless of whether you won't have intercourse, supports your physical and close to home bond.

3. Start sex and start to lead the pack incidentally. (A) Show him that you're excited and you need him. Keep in mind: feeling wanted is vital for men's sexual fulfillment. Assuming he's generally the person who starts sex, he has absolutely no chance of knowing whether you truly need it or simply oblige it when he brings it up. Embrace the weakness that accompanies getting this show on the road not knowing whether he'll respond.

• There are ways you can slide into this in the event that you're somewhat timid about starting. For instance, you could send him a prodding message like, I could have something special for you this evening in the room... in the event that you're available.

• Sending a provocative photograph can likewise attempt to start off something sexual. For instance, you could tie a lace around yourself, message him an image, and say, "You have a present... in any case, you need to open up it.

• This is likewise an effective method for working on your own fulfillment. On the off chance that you're starting to lead the pack, you can show him precisely the way in which you like to be contacted.

4. Shock him with a quick in and out on occasion. (A) A quick in and out lets him know you need him so severely you should have him at this moment. The most ideal way to start an unexpected quick in and out is to get him when he'd ordinarily be down for sex however isn't anticipating it right now. Then, at that point, simply begin making out with him and let things go from there.

• For instance, in the event that he loves morning sex, you could set your caution for 10 minutes ahead of schedule and wake him up with kisses and delicate strokes of his body.

• You can likewise start a quick in and out with a text. For instance, on the off chance that you're at home and realize he has a mid-day break coming up, you could message him, I have an exceptional lunch for you... in any case, you'll need to get back home to get it." When he gets back home, you can be holding up exposed or in some unmentionables he loves.

5. Speak profanely in bed. (A) Men frequently get excited and feel more wanted when you speak profanely. On the off chance that this isn't something you feel very alright with, begin with vaguer, PG-appraised remarks, for example, "I love when you put your hand there," or "You feel better." You can constantly slope it up from that point.

• Recollect that he needs to feel wanted, so center around what you love about him and cause it to seem like you can't get enough of him. For instance, you could say, "Your body against mine makes me so hot," or "I can't get enough of how you feel inside me."

• However long you're both alright with it, have a go at watching porn together to get a few smart thoughts for messy talk.

6. Show him that you're turned on. (A) At the point when he raises a ruckus around town spot, let him in on it. This doesn't imply that you want to groan and shout. There are alternate ways you can show that he's encouraging you: your muscles straining, getting him or a close by object, daintily scratching him, or breathing heavily.

• Go ahead and utilize your words too! For instance, you could say, "That feels better" or "I love when that's what you do" or "Kindly don't stop."

• Assuming that you have a vagina, know that faking climaxes isn't helping anybody. Best case scenario, all you do is instruct him that anything he was doing was working when it certainly wasn't.

7. Explore different avenues regarding new things. (A) Assortment makes your sexual coexistence more tomfoolery and agreeable. While this could incorporate exploring different avenues regarding unusual things, it's more about releasing your fun-loving side. Treat sex as a thrilling action that you and your accomplice both take part in and be watching out for various ways you can make it considerably more tomfoolery.

• There's science behind this, as well. Numerous examinations show that couples who really try to attempt new and various things in the room report more elevated levels of sexual longing and more noteworthy sexual fulfillment.

• In any event, attempting an alternate situation for penetrative sex could lead you to find new sentiments and vibes that you both truly appreciate.

• Go ahead and fall flat at something. For instance, many individuals explore different avenues regarding pretend to enliven their sexual experiences. In any case, here's the thing about pretend: It's very difficult to do convincingly! You could wind up imploding in an attack of laughs — and that is not a problem. It simply offers you one more opportunity to bond with one another.

8. Present a few props or toys. (A) Toys and props can help you both find out about your sexual reaction. Toys that vibrate function admirably to show you how you become stirred and answer various degrees of excitement. You can likewise attempt a blindfold for tactile hardship or a fur-shrouded paddle for some light effect play.

• On the off chance that you have a modest or apprehensive outlook on strolling into a physical sex shop, simply shop on the web. You don't for a moment even need to go to a sex-explicit site — major internet-based retailers, for example, Amazon likewise sell sex toys and props.

• You don't need to go out to shop all things considered! You can transform anything you have lying around the house into a sex toy (simply ensure its spotless first). For instance, you could attach your accomplice to the bed with bowties and bother him with a quill. Go sluggish so have opportunity and energy to see every one of the different erogenous zones on his body.

9. Take part in pad talk after sex. (A) Pad talk increments closeness and sexual fulfillment. The science behind pad talk is that having a climax floods your framework with oxytocin, a chemical that gives you warm, fluffy sensations of affection and trust. It makes you need to open up to your accomplice and offer your contemplations and sentiments.

• A recent report showed having more cushion talk brings about men explicitly feeling happier with their connections. So, if you have any desire to keep your significant other physically fulfilled, take a stab at saying romantic things to him after sex. Let him know how incredible he was and the way that astounding he causes you to feel.

10.Have open discussions about sex routinely. (A) Concentrates on show more prominent correspondence is related with additional climaxes. Couples who have open discussions about sex consistently wind up having really fulfilling sex thus. It additionally turns out they will generally engage in sexual relations all the more frequently too (maybe on the grounds that it's more normal on their brains).

• For instance, you could move toward your significant other and express, "This evening after supper, I'd like us to plunk down and discuss our sexual coexistence and how we can make it shockingly better than it as of now is."

• On the off chance that things aren't really going that extraordinary, you could say, "I know our sexual coexistence isn't really amazing. Might we at any point discuss it? Your fulfillment means a lot to me."

• Sex is a "no" or "prohibited" theme in a ton of societies and networks, so it's reasonable that you could have a modest or humiliated outlook on this from the start. Simply recollect that this is your better half.

Inside the holiness of marriage, it's great to discuss your sexual relationship.

11. Characterize what every one of you needs and needs physically. (A) Plunk down together and examine your sexual coexistence exhaustively. Pick when you can be separated from everyone else together. Get a beverage on the off chance that you need and open dependent upon one another about what's working for yourself as well as what's not. You could try and make a rundown out of unambiguous necessities and needs.

• For instance, you could list "climax" as one of your necessities. Then, at that point, you could examine with him how frequently you ordinarily climax when you two have intercourse and what explicit things assist with getting you there. To get some margin to ponder this and compose a rundown, that is fine. Be that as it may, don't simply hand your rundowns to one another to peruse quietly plunk down together and discuss them.

12. Work on giving and getting useful analysis. (A) Sandwich analysis between two commendations to relax the blow. We should be genuine

no one jumps at the chance to hear that they're not marvelous in bed. In any case, in the event that you and your better half are having a discussion about sex, the things you could do without will come up.

• For instance, you could say, "I truly love when you contact me. In the event that you involved your tongue too, it would truly take me over the top. That would make our sex considerably more astounding than it as of now is.

• Everyone likes various things in bed, there's no "one size fits all" with regards to sex. Recollect that your significant other is a definitive power of what satisfies him. On the off chance that you maintain that he should be physically fulfilled, what he says is a higher priority than what you've perused in a magazine, found in a video, or finished with different men.

• To acknowledge this sort of analysis, you need to permit yourself to be powerless and that can be intense. You could want to get guarded, yet attempt to have sympathy for your significant other and see things according to his perspective.

• Tolerating his analysis and making changes to more readily satisfy him additionally causes him to feel more wanted. You're showing him that you're physically drawn to him and need to satisfy him.

13. Get some information about his dreams. (A) Dreams help stimulate and energize you intellectually and genuinely. Before you begin sharing dreams, concur that you won't pass judgment on one another. Having a dream doesn't imply that you really believe should accomplish something, all things considered, yet it can act as a leaping off highlight investigate various thoughts and situations.

• For instance, assuming that he has a "hot medical caretaker" dream, you could find a provocative attendant's ensemble that you can wear a chance to assist with showcasing his dream. To lay everything out, you could begin by messaging him an image of the ensemble spread out on the bed and offer something like, "Would you say you are prepared for your actual this evening? I intend to give you an exhaustive assessment."

• Don't hesitate for even a moment to share your own dreams too. Numerous men will appreciate satisfying your dreams however much you appreciate satisfying theirs.

• You could try and find that you share a few dreams for all intents and purpose. For instance, you could have a dream of being restricted and defenseless, and he could have a dream of safeguarding a "lady in trouble." Those two dreams can cooperate!

•You can impart your considerations and sentiments to one another.

•Attempt to set aside a few minutes for having some good times together.

•Really try to be lively and track down something that works for you two as a couple.

14. Focus on sex in your lives. (A) In reality, booking sex can assist you with expanding the recurrence. Planning for sex on your schedule could sound truly un-hot, yet it shows that sex is similarly as essential to you as different things you set aside a few minutes for. It additionally holds different things back from hindering engaging in sexual relations.

• Planning a particular time for sex expects you to plan different things around it, instead of the opposite way around. This is something extraordinary to attempt assuming you find that sex continues to get pushed to the side for different things you really want to do.

• This doesn't actually intend that, when the opportunity arrives, you must have sex regardless of whether you need to. Your drive could not necessarily in every case coordinate with your schedule and that is totally fine. All things being equal, invest that energy unwinding and holding one another.

15.Work-out routinely to help your energy and moxie. (A) Actual work gives you more endurance and better flow. Actual excitement relies an extraordinary arrangement upon great blood stream, so further developing your course straightforwardly further develops your sexual coexistence. Aside from that, more grounded and better bodies are more equipped for getting a charge out of sexual movement overall (as well as remaining at it longer).

• Becoming more grounded and all the more in great shape additionally works on your self-idea and mental self-portrait, which one review showed is straightforwardly connected with both climax and sex drive or sexual craving.

• Kegel works out, which reinforce your pelvic floor muscles, have sexual advantages for all kinds of people. To find your pelvic floor muscles, fix or secure like you're attempting to hold back from passing gas. Contract these muscles for 3-5 seconds, then, at that point, discharge for 3-5 seconds. Rehash this cycle multiple times.

16. Keep up with individual leisure activities and interests. (A) Doing all that together can make your accomplice excessively recognizable. On the off chance that you and your significant other have no independence in your relationship, you can neglect to focus on yourselves as people. At the point when that's what you do, concentrates on show, your energy and sexual craving for one another begin to diminish. You can hold this back from occurring by ensuring that every one of you has your own things that you truly do isolate from one another.

• For instance, you could each take a different class one night seven days, or join rec association groups in various games. Parting ways can be similarly pretty much as significant as hanging out.

• Moreover, it turns out the well-known adage that "nonappearance causes the heart to become fonder" really holds some reality. At the point when your accomplice's nowhere to be found, your

creative mind kicks in and they become more attractive — so you could design solo end of the week escapes, then prepare for a hot get-together.

17. Attempt a sex specialist in the event that you experience difficulty conveying. (A) Sex specialists assist you with discussing sex in a useful, significant way. On the off chance that you've attempted a few thoughts sexual fulfillment actually appears to be barely unattainable; a sex specialist could possibly help. They'll ask you inquiries intended to get to the foundation of your issues with closeness so you can connect with one another physically in a seriously satisfying manner.

• Conjugal or couples' advisors can likewise assist you with taking care of problems that you're having, yet they generally don't zero in explicitly on sex. A sex specialist, then again, begins with your sexual relationship and works outward from that.

• It's normal to have an off-kilter outlook on going to a specialist or discussing such private points. A decent specialist will assist with making you feel relaxed so you feel open to conversing with them.

18. Seek clinical treatment for sexual brokenness. (A) Issues with excitement are normal and nothing to be embarrassed about. May individuals will encounter a sexual brokenness eventually in their lives of some kind. It very well may be a characteristic piece of maturing, a side effect of a different clinical issue, or a symptom of a medicine you're taking. On the off chance that you converse with a specialist about the thing you're encountering, they can assist with deciding the reason and figure out how to help.

• For instance, assuming you experience sexual brokenness as a result of a prescription you're taking, your primary care physician could possibly recommend you an alternate drug that will treat the very condition without that incidental effect.

- Chemical medicines can help the two individuals who are encountering a deficiency of charisma or decreased sex drive.

SECTION 3

The Astounding Medical advantages of Sex

The advantages of sex range from slicing feelings of anxiety to bringing down your gamble of disease and coronary failures. Sex works with holding and sensations of closeness with your accomplice. This sort of connectedness accomplishes more than cause you to feel warm and fluffy, it really decreases tension and lifts your general wellbeing.

How might you like a more grounded resistant framework or better rest? Activity between the sheets can assist you with getting all of this and that's only the tip of the iceberg.

1. Get Less Colds and Lift Your Resistant Framework

More sex approaches less days off. That is the very thing the aftereffects of studies contrasting physically dynamic individuals with the people who are not physically dynamic say. Sex supports your body's capacity to make defensive antibodies against microbes, infections, and different microorganisms that cause normal diseases. Obviously, there's something else to developing a vigorous invulnerable framework besides having a sound sexual coexistence. Eating right, working out, getting satisfactory rest, and staying up with the latest with inoculations all add to serious areas of strength for having sound protections against infectious ailments.

2. Support Your Moxie

In all honesty, the best remedy for a disappearing drive is to engage in sexual relations! Engaging in sexual relations really supports want. Also, in the event that aggravation and vaginal dryness make it trying for certain ladies to have intercourse, sexual movement can assist with combatting these issues, as well. Sex helps vaginal oil, blood stream to the vagina, and versatility of the tissues, all of which make for better, more pleasurable sex and elevated moxie.

3. Further develop Ladies' Bladder Control

Urinary incontinence influences around 30% of ladies sooner or later throughout everyday life. Having normal climaxes works a lady's pelvic floor muscles, fortifying and conditioning them. Climaxes enact the very muscles that ladies use while doing Kegel works out. Having more grounded pelvic muscles implies there's less gamble of mishaps and pee spills.

4. Bring down Your Circulatory strain

Could it be said that you are one of the large numbers of individuals who experience the ill effects of hypertension? Sex can assist you with bringing down it. Many examinations have reported a connection between intercourse explicitly (not masturbation) and lower systolic circulatory strain, the main number that shows up on a pulse test. That is uplifting news for people searching for a simple assistant to way of life (diet, work out, stress decrease) and medicine techniques to get pulse into a sound reach. Sex meetings can't supplant circulatory strain bringing drugs down to control hypertension, however they might be a valuable expansion.

5. Considers Exercise

Like each and every other sort of actual work, sex consumes calories, as well! Sitting and staring at the television consumes around 1 calorie each moment. Engaging in sexual relations builds your pulse and uses different muscle gatherings, consuming around 5 calories each moment.

Normal sex can't supplant meetings at the rec center, yet a having a functioning, solid sexual coexistence is a decent method for getting some extra actual work.

6. Lower Coronary failure Chance

Need a better heart? Have more sex. Sexual action helps keep levels of chemicals, similar to estrogen and testosterone, within proper limits. With regards to safeguarding heart wellbeing by having intercourse, more is better. One concentrate in men showed that the people who had intercourse no less than 2 times each week were half less inclined to pass on from coronary illness than their less physically dynamic friends.

7. Reduce Agony

Sexual excitement (counting masturbation) and climax can assist with keeping torment under control. The two exercises can decrease torment sensation and increment your aggravation limit. Climaxes bring

about the arrival of chemicals that can assist with hindering agony signals. A few ladies report that self-excitement through masturbation can decrease side effects of feminine spasms, joint pain, and even migraine.

8. May Lessen Prostate Disease Hazard

There are male-explicit medical advantages of sex, as well. One review showed that men who had incessant discharges (characterized as 21 times each month or more) were less inclined to foster prostate malignant growth than the people who had less discharges. It didn't make any difference assuming that the discharges happened through intercourse, masturbation, or nighttime outflows. Obviously, there's something else to prostate malignant growth risk besides recurrence of discharges, however this was one fascinating finding.

9. Further develop Rest

Sex can assist you with resting better. Prolactin advances sensations of unwinding and drowsiness. This is only one reason you might see that you make some simpler memories nodding off in the wake of engaging in sexual relations.

10. Ease Pressure

Sex is an extraordinary pressure reliever. That is on the grounds that contacting, embracing, sexual closeness, and profound connection invigorate the arrival of "inspirational" substances that advance holding and serenity. Sexual excitement additionally delivers substances that animate the award and joy framework in the mind. Encouraging closeness and closeness can assist with easing tension and lift in general wellbeing.

11. Consume Calories

One concentrate in young fellows and ladies showed that sex consumes around 108 calories each half hour! That is sufficient to consume off 3, 570 calories.

12. Work on Cardiovascular Wellbeing

Better cardiovascular wellbeing might be essentially as close as the room. While certain individuals might stress that actual effort from sex might prompt a stroke, science proposes in any case. In a 20-extended investigation of in excess of 900 men, scientists found that recurrence of sex didn't increment stroke risk. They found that sex safeguards against deadly cardiovascular failures, as well. Men who had intercourse something like two times seven days diminished their gamble of a lethal cardiovascular failure by half contrasted with gentlemen who engaged in sexual relations not exactly one time per month.

13. Fortify Your Prosperity

People are wired for social association. Connection with loved ones supports your general wellbeing and prosperity. Close associations with others, including your accomplice, make you more joyful and better contrasted with the people who are less very much associated. Studies demonstrate it!

14. Further develop Closeness and Connections

You can embrace and nestle your method for growing warm, close connections. Sex and climaxes invigorate the arrival of a chemical called oxytocin that assists individuals with holding. This "adoration chemical" as it's usually known, helps construct sensations of affection and trust. In an investigation of premenopausal ladies, the additional time the women spent canoodling and embracing their spouses or accomplices, the higher their oxytocin levels were.

15. Look More youthful

Customary sex invigorates the arrival of estrogen and testosterone, chemicals that keep you youthful and crucial looking. Estrogen advances more youthful looking skin and radiant locks. In one review, passes judgment on saw members through a one-way reflect and speculated their ages. Individuals who engaged in sexual relations no less than 4 times each week with a customary accomplice were seen to be 7 to 12 years more youthful than they really were.

16. Live Longer

What's the key to living longer? It could be having more sex. In a very long-term investigation of more than 1,000 moderately aged men, the people who had the most climaxes had a portion of the demise pace of the people who didn't discharge much of the time. Obviously, many variables add to life span, however having a functioning sexual coexistence might be a simple, pleasurable method for broadening your life expectancy.

17. Support Mental ability

The advantages of sex genuinely stretch out from head to toe. A functioning sexual coexistence could really make your mind work better. Specialists found that sex switches the cerebrum into a more insightful method of and thinking handling. What's more, creature studies recommend that sex upgrades region of the mind engaged with memory.

18. Sex Makes Treatment More straightforward

A review performed at a ripeness place found that men who had day to day discharges for seven days had more excellent sperm than the individuals who didn't discharge every day. Men in the day-to-day discharge bunch had sperm with DNA that was less divided than the DNA from sperm of men who discharged less regularly. Less divided DNA infers better DNA. Also, generous sperm that have sound DNA are bound to treat an egg.

www.ingramcontent.com/pod-product-compliance
Lightning Source LLC
LaVergne TN
LVHW020533160826
845677LV00015B/4026
9798848190502